PIANO FOR BEGINNERS LEARN TO PLAY *MORE* CHRISTMAS CAROLS

A BEGINNER PIANO SHEET MUSIC
SONGBOOK FOR KIDS AND ADULTS
WITH 30 HOLIDAY FAVORITES

Producer & International Distributor
eBookPro Publishing
www.ebook-pro.com

Piano for Beginners
Learn to Play More Christmas Carols

Made Easy Press

Copyright © 2024 Made Easy Press

All rights reserved; No parts of this book may be reproduced or transmitted in any form or by any means, electronic or mechanical, including photocopying, recording, taping, or by any information retrieval system, without the author's explicit permission in writing.

Transcribed by Asti Fajriani

Contact: agency@ebook-pro.com
ISBN **9789655754162**

CONTENTS

INTRODUCTION 6

HOW TO USE THIS BOOK 7

GET TO KNOW YOUR PIANO 8

RECOGNIZING KEYS 9

READING MUSIC 10

UNDERSTANDING NOTE LENGTHS 11

RESTS 13

SHARPS AND FLATS 14

MORE NOTATIONS 15

PLAYING WITH BOTH HANDS 17

GETTING STARTED 20

    All Glory, Laud, and Honor *21*

    All Hail the Power of Jesus' Name *22*

Angels from the Realm of Glory..................23

Blessed Assurance..........................24

Christ the Lord is Risen Today..................25

Come, Thou Almighty King....................26

Come, Thou Long-Expected Jesus..............27

Faith of Our Fathers..........................28

For the Beauty of the Earth....................29

God Rest Ye Merry Gentlemen.................30

He Leadeth Me............................. 31

How Great Our Joy..........................32

I Need Thee Every Hour......................33

Jesus Paid It All.............................34

Joyful, Joyful, We Adore Thee..................35

Just a Closer Walk With Thee..................36

Just As I Am................................37

Make Me a Blessing.........................38

Mary, Did You Know?........................39

Now I Belong to Jesus........................40

One Small Child............................ 41

Onward Christian Soldiers....................42

Praise to the Lord, the Almighty................43

Since I Have Been Redeemed 44

Speak, O Lord 45

Sun of My Soul 46

The Birthday of a King 47

The Joy of the Lord is My Strength 48

Trust and Obey 49

Were You There 50

APPENDIX A – CHORDS 51

INTRODUCTION

Welcome to your second Christmas Carols piano book!

The perfect addition to How to Play Christmas Carols, this second book has 30 brand-new seasonal and festive songs accompanied by an introductory lesson on the basics of reading notes, to refresh your memory.

So dive in to this whole new collection of carols and extend your piano-playing repertoire just in time for the holiday season!

HOW TO USE THIS BOOK

First, read the Get to Know Your Piano section.

This short guide will remind you of the fundamentals of reading notes, after which, and with a little practice, any beginning musician will be able to read and play all the music in this collection.

As this is meant to be a First Piano Book, all the songs can be played with one hand. For more advanced learners, we have included chords that can be played with the left hand as well, simultaneously. You will find an explanation for playing chords in Appendix A.

GET TO KNOW YOUR PIANO

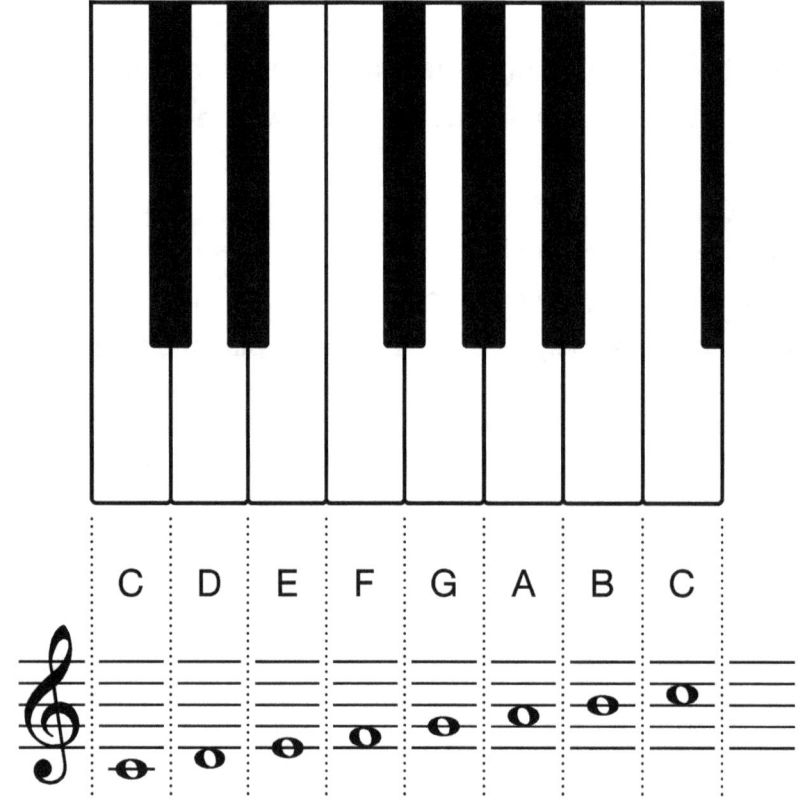

RECOGNIZING KEYS

A piano is made up of **keys**, each of which makes a different sound – called a **note**.

A piano has white keys and black keys – we call the white ones by their letters, from A-G – just like you can see in the picture.

You will notice that the black keys come in groups – first two, then three, and so on.

Look at your piano – and put your finger on the C note. You will recognize it as the white key immediately on the left of the group of two black keys. You will notice that there are several different C keys on your keyboard – we'll always start with the one closest to the middle.

From there, going to your right, play each white note, one at a time – C, D, E, F, G, A, B – just like in the picture.

The more you practice, the easier it will be to recognize the notes – but for now, just remember where the C key is, and work from there!

READING MUSIC

Now, look at the five lines with the swirly symbol on the left. This is a **Treble Clef** which indicates the beginning of a new line of music.

Musical notes are drawn on and between the lines, going from left to right, and now we will learn how to recognize them.

Find the C note on your piano again like we learned and look at how it looks on the lines. It is the only note with a line through it – and that is how we will remember it.

From there, the notes go higher up along the lines – with every consecutive note going up one half-line.

So after C comes D, which sits just below the first line. Next is E, which sits right on the middle of the first line – and so on.

The first few times you play, look back at the drawing to remind yourself which note goes where. Once you've practiced a few songs, you should remember them by heart more easily.

UNDERSTANDING NOTE LENGTHS

You will notice that some music notes are black, others are white, some have lines and some only ovals, and others are connected together with beams. All of these things help us understand how long we should keep our finger on the note before we go on to the next one.

This is a **quarter note**. It is the most common and the simplest. Put your finger on one of the piano keys and play a short note – count in your head or out loud to one, and then let go.

This is a **half note**. This note is **twice as long** as a regular note. This time, count to 2 before you let go.

This note is **even longer**, and you'll usually find it at the end of a line or song. It is called a **whole note**. Count to 4 before you move on to the next one.

This note is an 8th note – it is only **half as long** as a quarter note. Press the key once and don't hold your finger on it for long.

Whenever you see a dotted note, like these:

That means you must play for slightly longer than the regular length of the note. So, for example, a dotted quarter note (black with a straight line) will be played slightly longer than a regular quarter note, but less long than a half note.

When you see notes connected with a **beam**, like this:

That means you have to play the notes quickly, one after the other, without pausing in between.

You'll notice that each song has the lyrics written underneath, telling you exactly what to sing for every note.

So, you can also use your knowledge of the songs in the book to help you understand how long each note should be.

You'll notice that there are some capital letters above the music lines. These letters tell us what we should play with our left hand – and they are called chords. You can play all the songs in this book with your right hand only, or with both hands – this is a more advanced skill.

When you feel like you've mastered playing with your right hand, head over to Appendix A at the end of this book where you will find instructions on playing chords with your left hand.

RESTS

This symbol is a rest:

It means take a break, and count in your head to one before you play the next note. It is the same length as a quarter note.

This is another rest symbol:

It is a shorter rest – take a break again, but this time, only wait half the time - as long as an 8th note.

If you see two notes connected between them with a tie, like this:

That means you shouldn't stop and lift your finger between both notes, but rather you should play them immediately one after the other.

SHARPS AND FLATS

The black keys on the piano are called *sharps* or *flats*, and they don't have their own names. **D sharp** means the black key to the **right** of D. **D flat** means the black key to the left of D.

A sharp is recognized by this symbol: ♯

While a flat is recognized by this one: ♭

So whenever you see one of these symbols on the music lines next to a note, you'll play the black key that is immediately next to that note – on its right if it is sharp ♯ or its left if it is flat ♭.

Sometimes, throughout the entire song one or two notes will always be sharps or flats. So, instead of putting a sharp or flat symbol next to every single note, we'll put the symbol once at the beginning of every line of music, right next to the Treble Clef, like this:

This is called a **Key Signature.**
In this example, whenever there is a B in the song, we'll make sure to play B flat – the black key immediately to the left of B.
Sometimes, we can have more than one sharp or flat in the song:

In this example, we can see that whenever there is a C or F in the song, we'll play C# or F# - in other words, the black key to the right of C or the black key to the right of F, accordingly.

MORE NOTATIONS

In level 1, we learned about note lengths.

This note:

This note is **the longest**, and you'll usually find it at the end of a line or at the very end of a song. It is called a **whole note**. Count to 4 before you move on to the next one.

If you see two notes connected between them with a tie, like this:

That means you shouldn't stop and lift your finger between both notes, but rather you should play them immediately one after the other.

This symbol is called a natural. Remember when we learned about sharps and flats, and key signatures?

Well, a **natural** temporarily cancels out a key signature. In other words, if you have a specific note which is always played sharp, or flat, once you see it with this symbol you must remember to play it in its regular form.

This note looks funny but it's actually simple! It's played just how it looks – both notes at the same time. So, in this example, you'll play F and G together for the length of a half note.

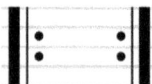

This is a repeat sign. If you see a section of music beginning and ending with repeat brackets, that means this section of the song is meant to be repeated. You will know from the lyrics just how many times the segment should be repeated.

A coda indicates a jump in the music. In the sheet music for Go Tell it On the Mountain, for example, you will see the coda symbol hovering above the final line of music. You can also see, in the middle of the second line of music, the phrase "To Coda". This means that during the final repetition of the music, should you choose to repeat the song, once you reach "To Coda", you must skip the next lines of music and pick up again where you see the coda symbol at the end of the song. This will ensure that the song gets a proper ending.

When you see an accent above or below a note, it means the particular note should be played louder, or stronger, than the other notes. Essentially, the accent does not change the length of the note, but rather its emphasis.

PLAYING WITH BOTH HANDS

Until now, in Level 1, all the music could be played with your right hand only.

In level 2 we will graduate to playing with both hands which will give the songs more life and, of course, increase their level of difficulty.

We recommend beginning by learning how to play a full song with the right hand, and only then incorporating the left hand as well.

In Level 1, we learned about the Treble Clef. That is the marking that indicates the beginning of a new line of music. More accurately, the Treble Clef indicates a line of music meant to be played with the fingers of your right hand.

When we play with both hands, we have two separate lines of music – one on top that begins with a Treble Clef, indicating the right hand, and another on the bottom that begins with a Bass Clef, indicating the left hand.

Both lines are meant to be played simultaneously – as you can see, the lyrics pertain to both lines of music, top and bottom.
In Level 1, we learned to recognize keys in Treble Clef (or, the top line of music).

The Bass Clef keys are recognized differently, with the different lines indicating different notes. The order of the notes is still the same — A, B, C, D, E, F, G — but their placing is different.

Take a look at this diagram:

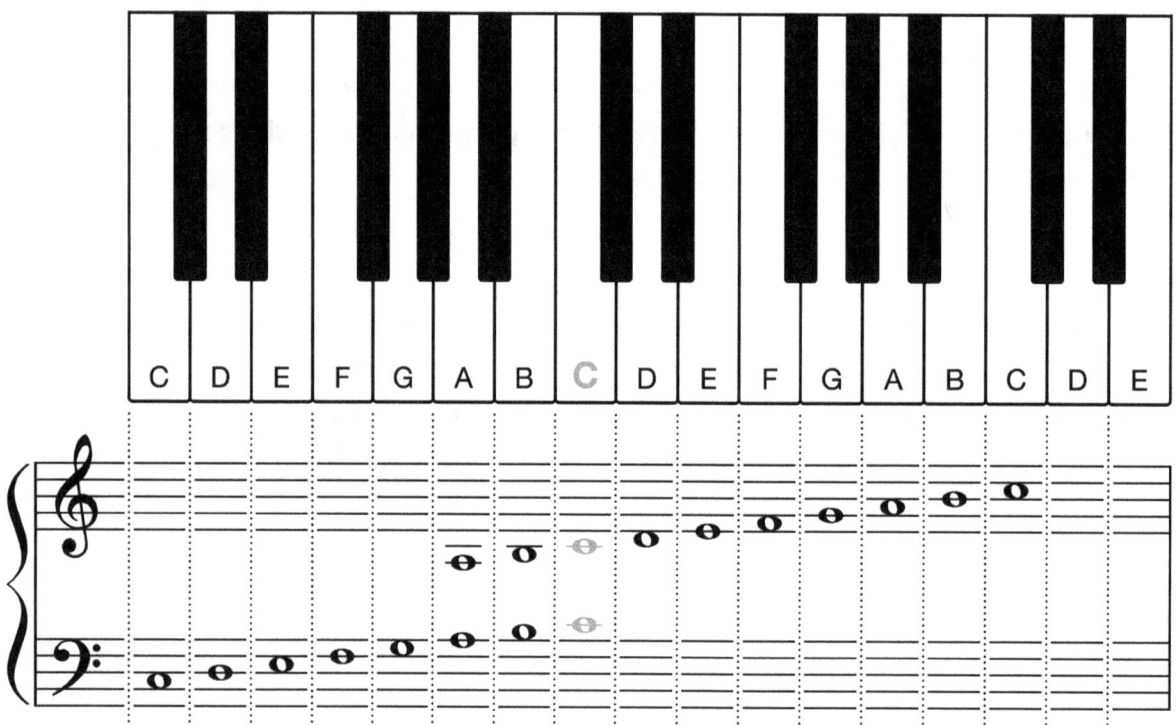

You will notice that the Treble Clef is a direct continuation of the Bass Clef — you will just have to learn a new method of recognizing the keys for your left hand.

A common way of remembering which note is which is by using these mnemonics, with each initial letter indicating where the notes are located on the five lines of the clef:

Every **G**ood **B**oy **D**oes **F**ine (Treble Clef) – the lowest line of music is E, then G, then B and so on.

Good **B**oys **D**o **F**ine **A**lways (Bass Clef) – the lowest line of music is G, then B, then D and so on. In the Bass Clef we will generally use the notes higher up on the lines, as you can see in the diagram.

Come back to this diagram to remind yourself while you're still figuring out the left hand.

GETTING STARTED

Let's look at this example of the first line of Baa Baa Black Sheep:

The numbers above the notes help show you which finger of your right hand to use when playing each note.

1 means use your thumb – and so on until 5, which is your pinky.

So in this example, you'd start with playing C twice with your thumb (remember, we read notes from left to right just like we read English), then G twice with your second finger, then A with your third, B with your fourth, C with your fifth, back again to A with your third and finally G with your second finger.

Try it – and sing along!

Remember, playing with the correct fingers is important and will help make sure you are playing the piano in the best possible way!

Congratulations! You've learned how to read music notes.
Now pick out a song and use what you've learned to make some beautiful music!

All Glory, Laud, and Honor

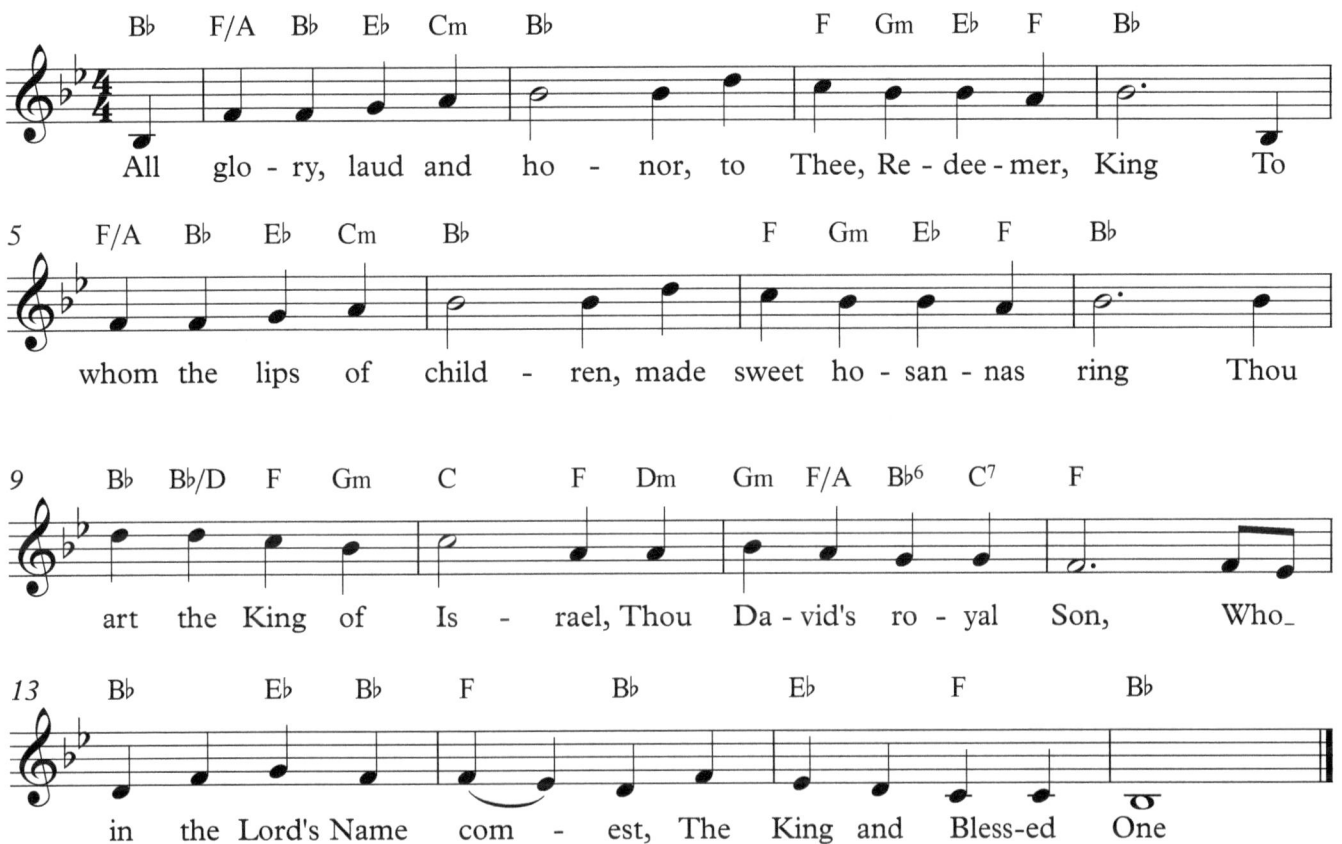

All Hail the Power of Jesus' Name

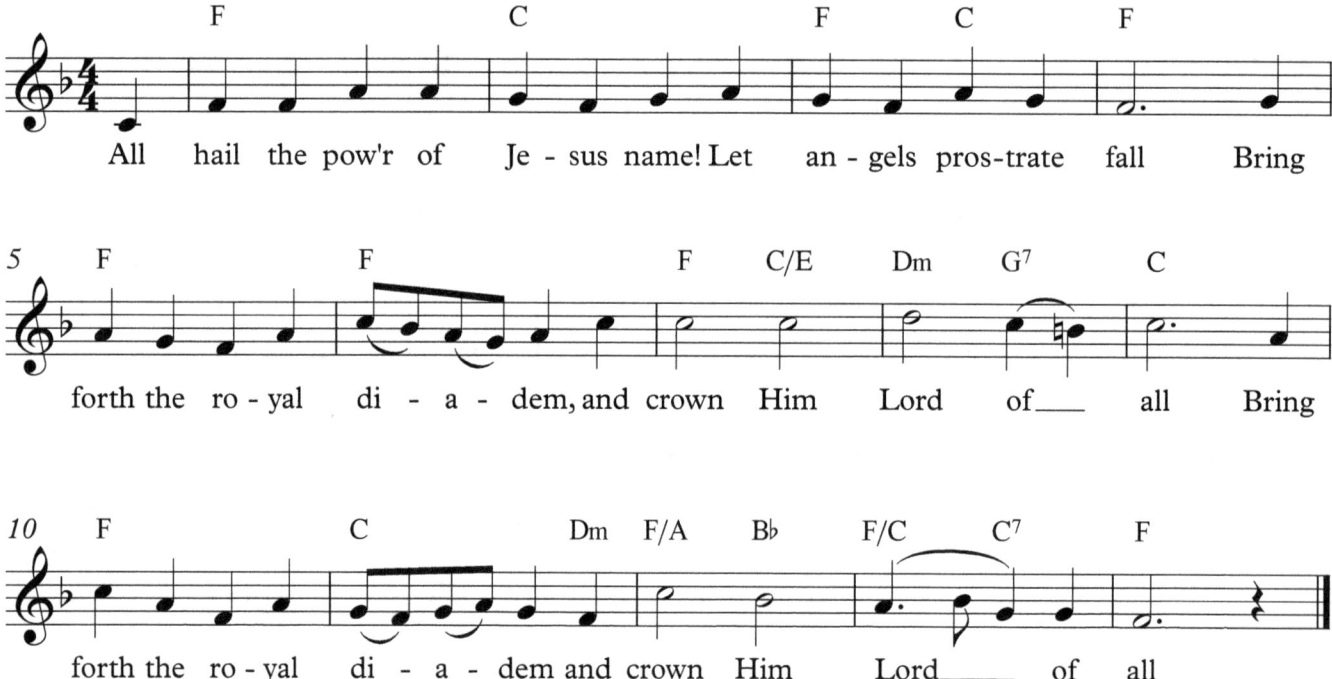

Angels from the Realms of Glory

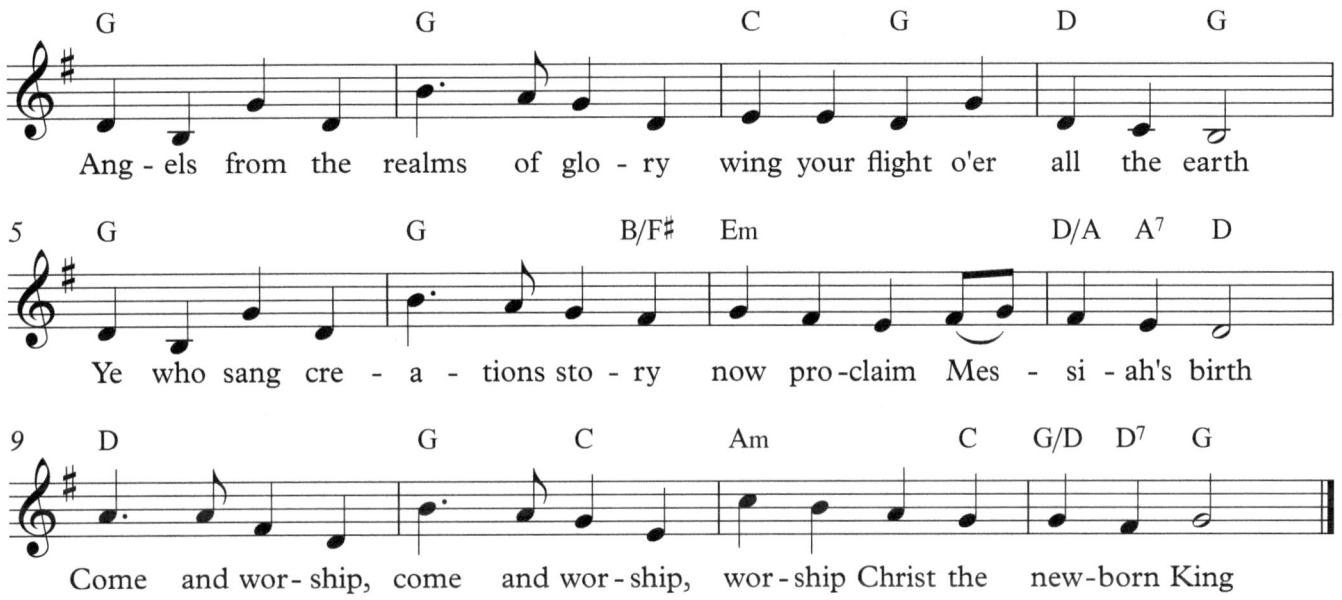

Blessed Assurance

Christ the Lord is Risen Today

Come, Thou Almighty King

Come, Thou Long-Expected Jesus

Faith of Our Fathers

For the Beauty of the Earth

God Rest Ye Merry Gentlemen

He Leadeth Me

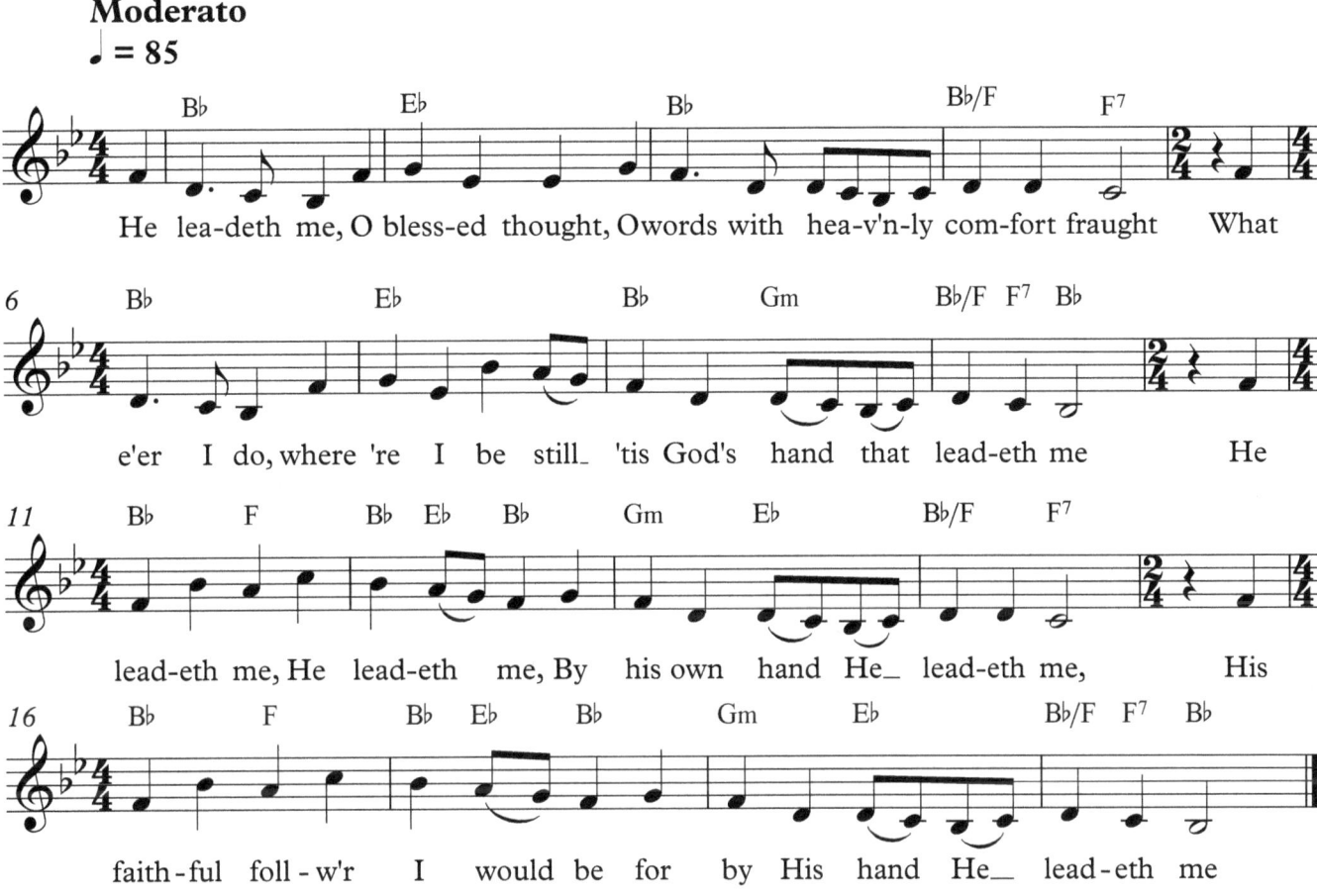

How Great Our Joy

I Need Thee Every Hour

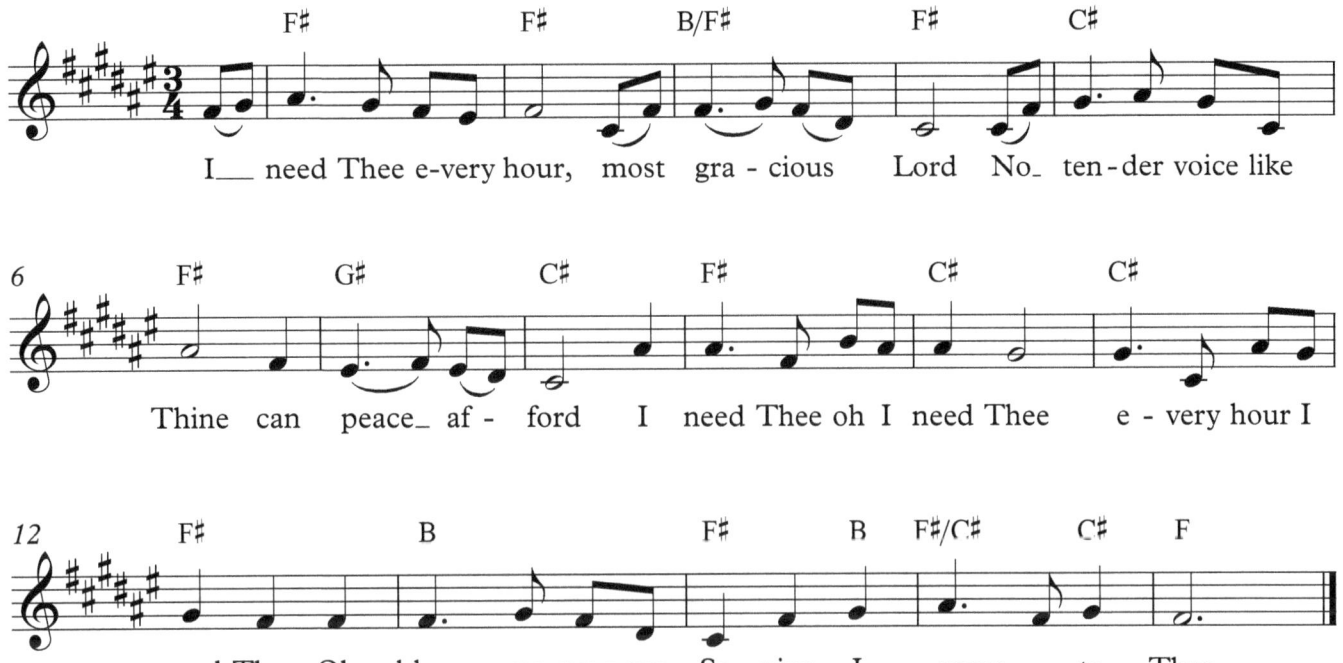

Jesus Paid It All

Joyful, Joyful, We Adore Thee

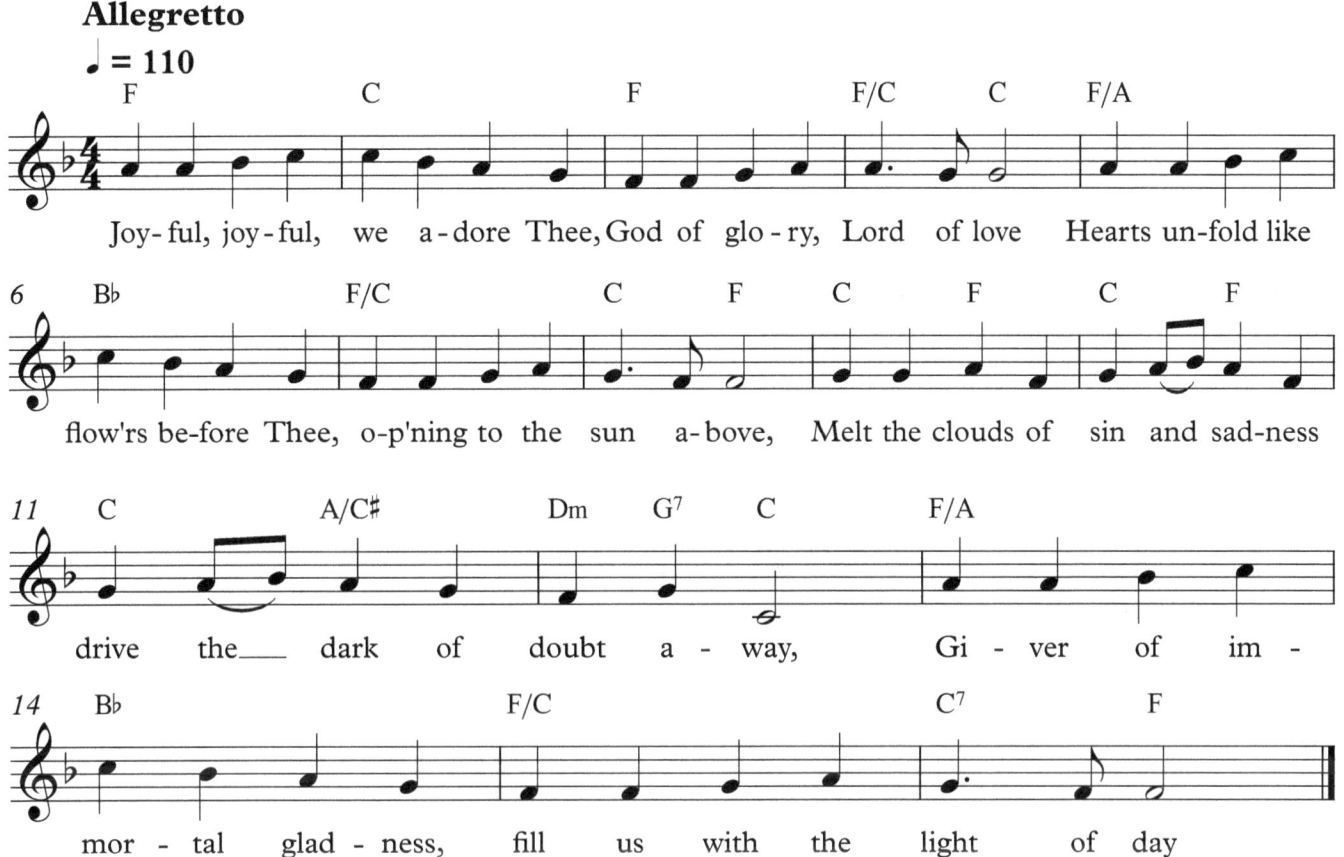

Just a Closer Walk with Thee

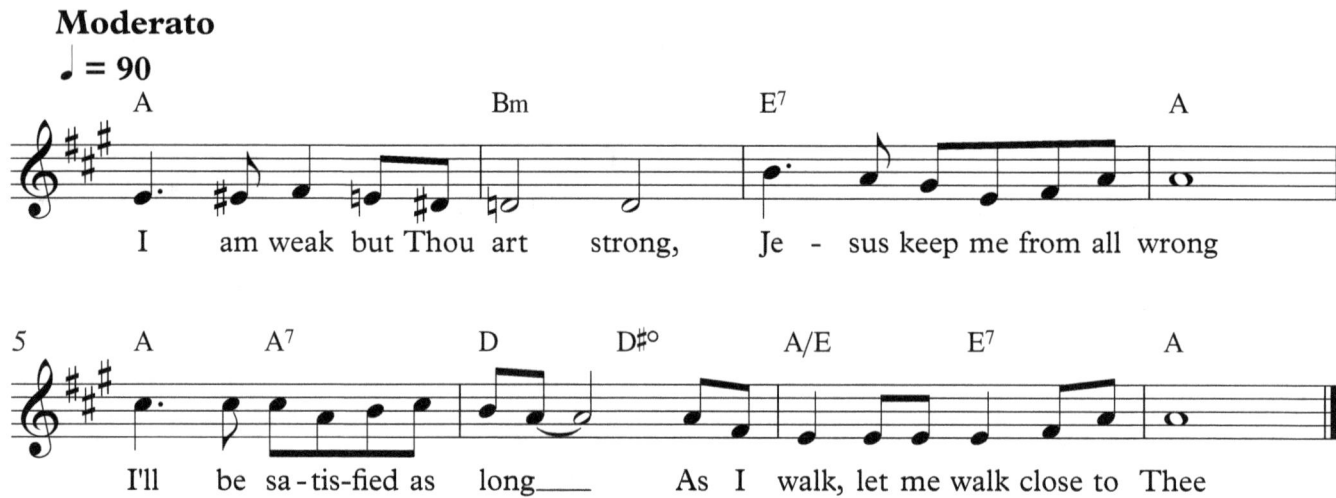

Just As I Am

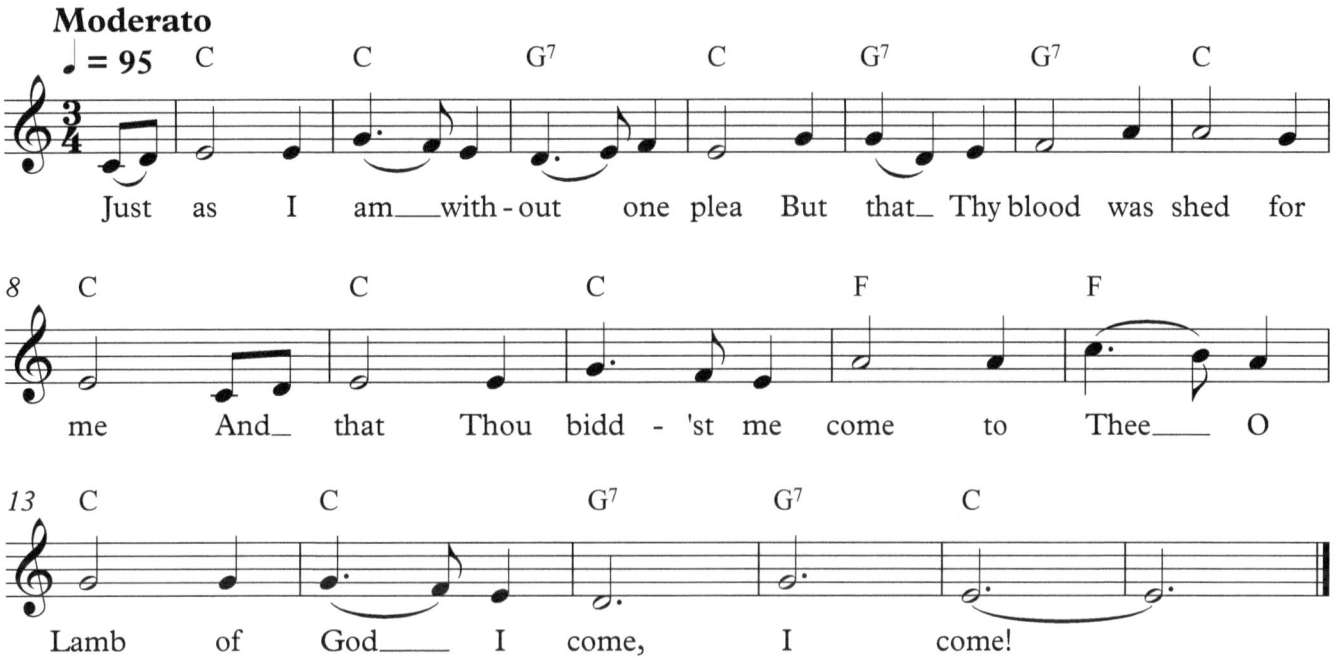

Make Me a Blessing

Mary, Did You Know?

Now I Belong to Jesus

One Small Child

Onward Christian Soldiers

Praise to the Lord, the Almighty

Since I Have Been Redeemed

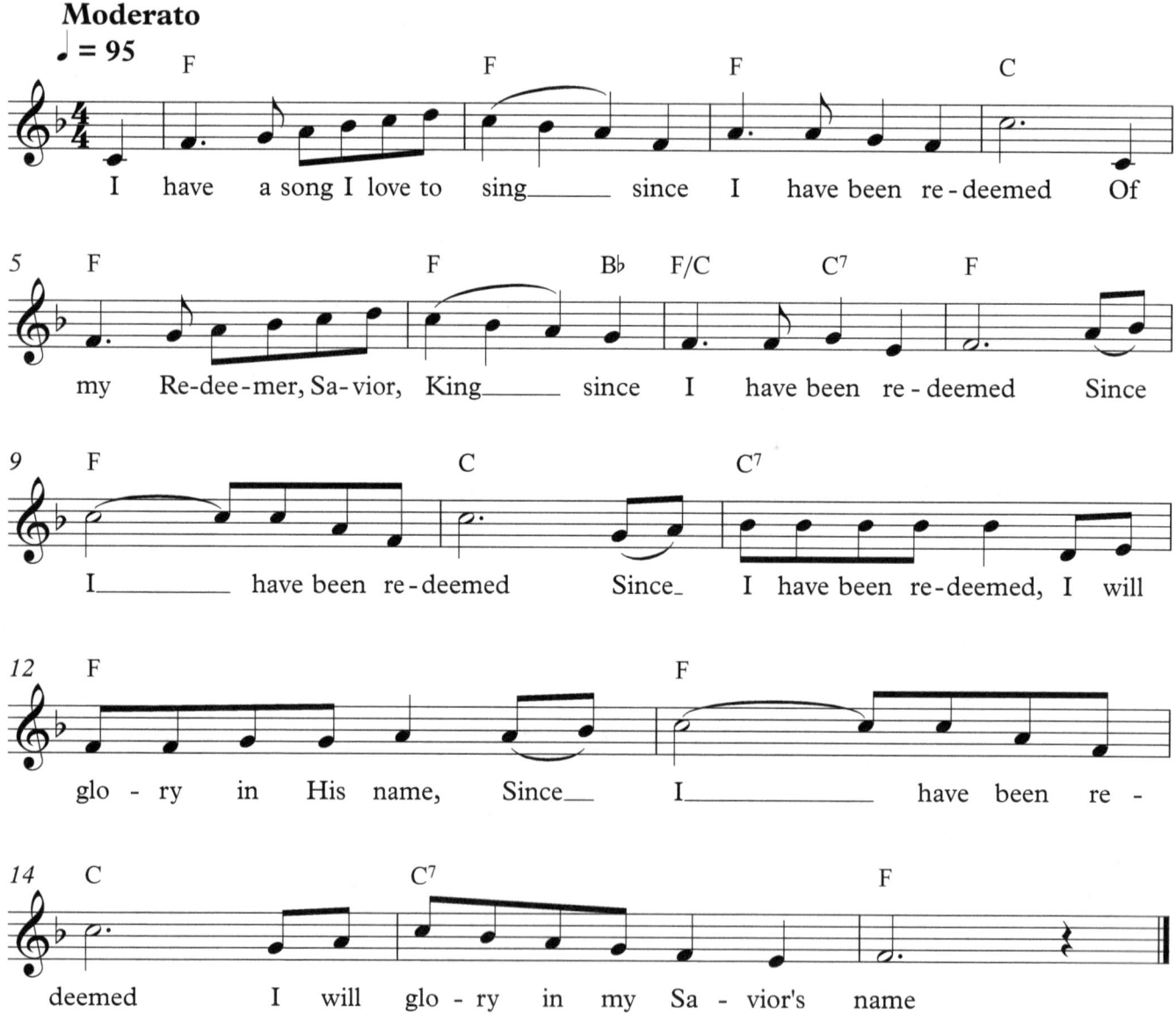

Speak, O Lord

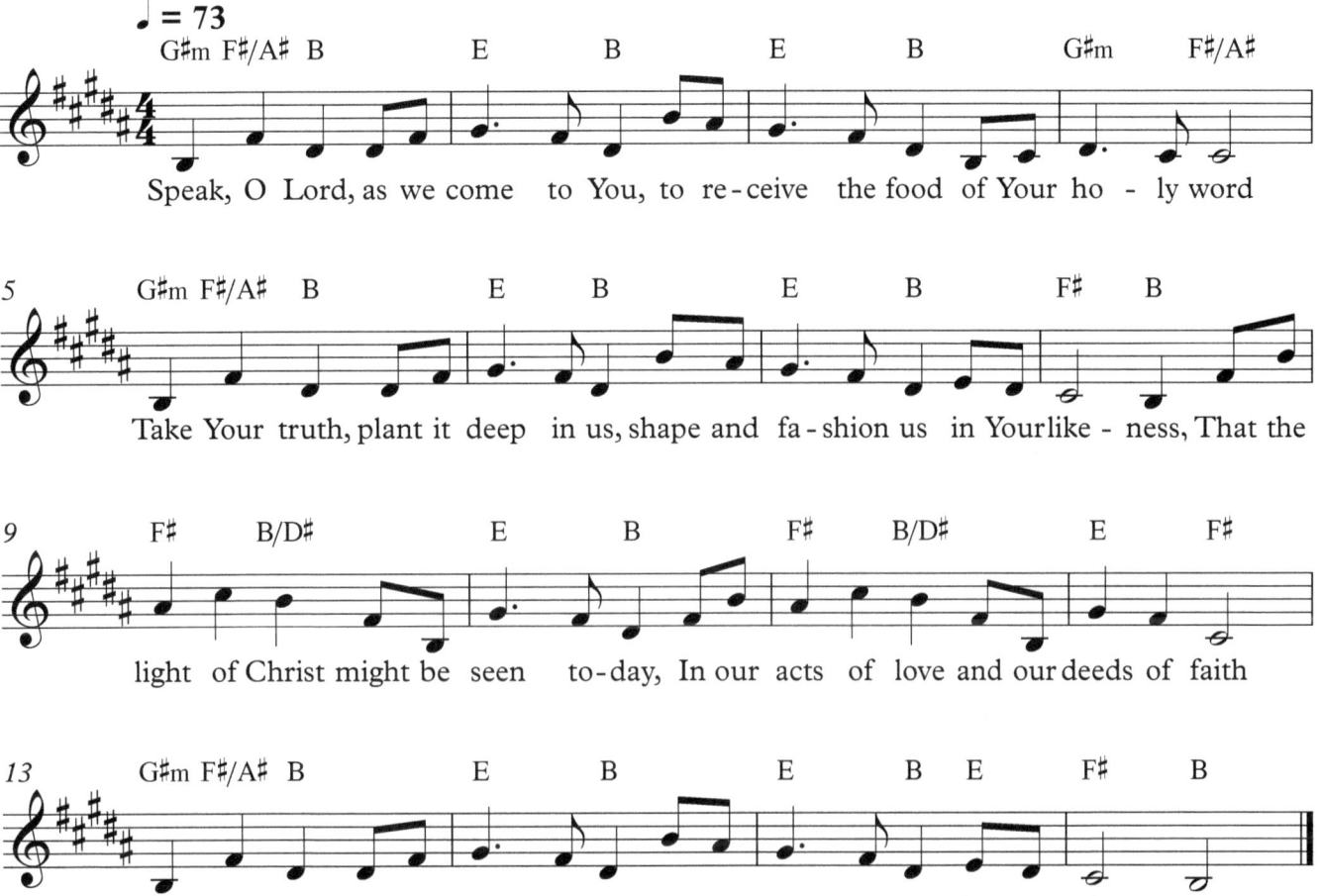

Sun of My Soul

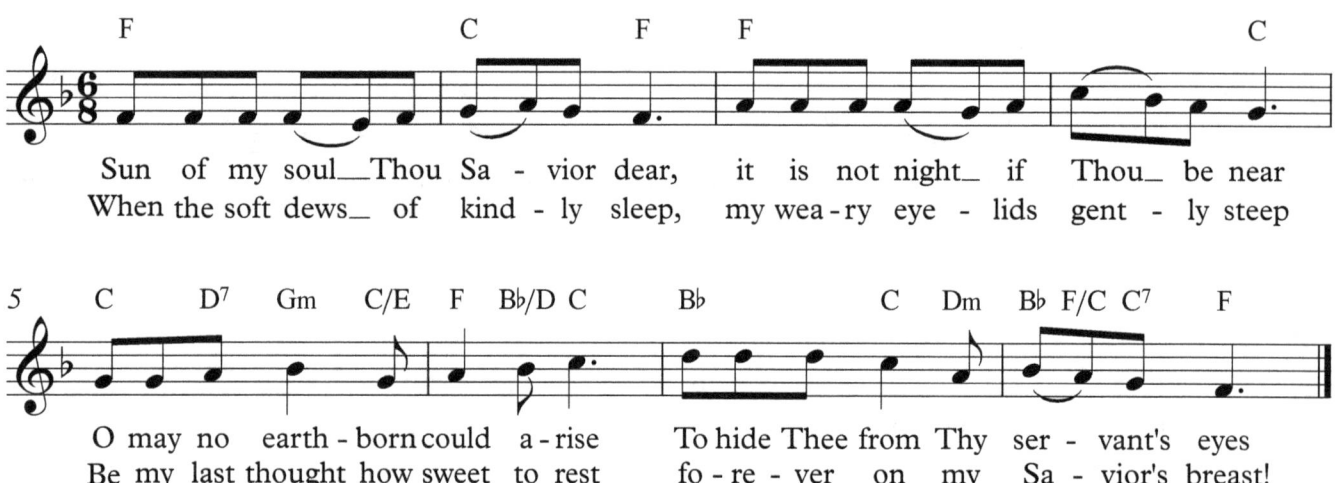

The Birthday of a King

The Joy of the Lord is My Strength

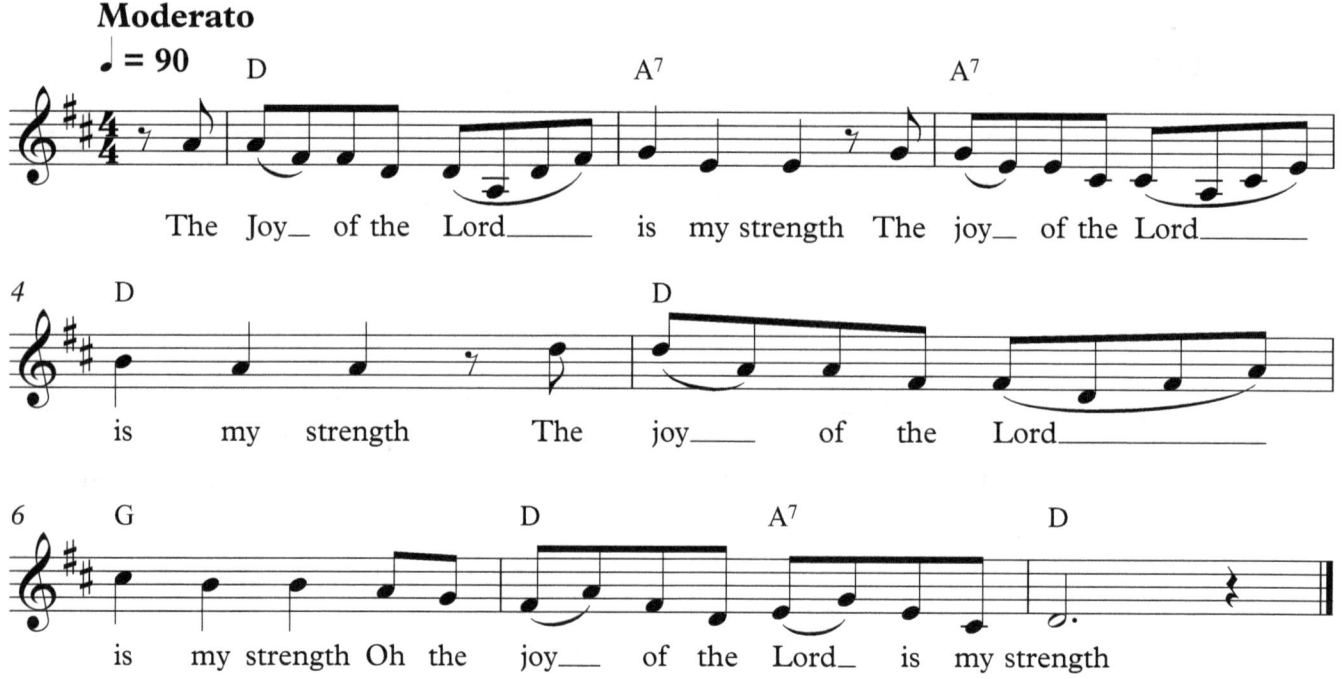

Trust and Obey

Were You There

APPENDIX A – CHORDS

Once you've learned to read and play notes with your right hand, you can go on to play with your left hand, too.

You'll notice that there are some capital letters above the music lines. These letters tell us what we should play with our left hand – and they are called chords.

Chords are a combination of three notes played at once, to accompany the melody being played with the right hand.

Chords are always played one octave lower than the melody!

PIANO CHORDS

KEY	MAJOR	MINOR	SEVENTH	AUGMENTED	DIMINISHED
A					
B					
C					
D					
E					
F					
G					

We hope you enjoyed

Piano for Beginners
Learn to Play
More Christmas Carols

We'd appreciate it so much if you would consider going to Amazon and leaving a review.

Your reviews help us bring you more fun, family-friendly content like this book.

About Made Easy Press

At *Made Easy Press*, our goal is to bring you beautifully designed, thoughtful gifts and products.

We strive to make complicated things – easy. Whether it's learning new skills or putting memories into words, our books are led by values of family, creativity, and self-care and we take joy in creating authentic experiences that make people truly happy.

Look out for other books
by Made Easy Press here!

www.ingramcontent.com/pod-product-compliance
Lightning Source LLC
LaVergne TN
LVHW081535070526
838199LV00006B/370